Contents

There are Buddhists all over the world. They follow the teachings of the Buddha.

EVERYDAY RELIGION

My Buddhist Life

Meg St. Pierre and Marty Casey

WAYLAND

EVERYDAY RELIGION

My Buddhist Life
My Christian Life
My Hindu Life
My Jewish Life
My Muslim Life
My Sikh Life

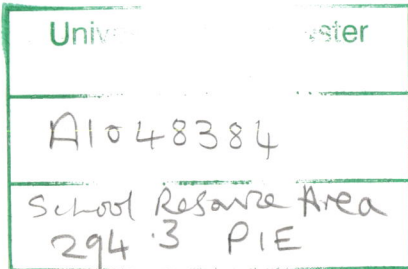

Editor: Ruth Raudsepp
Designer: Joyce Chester

First published in 1996 by Wayland Publishers Limited, 61 Western Road,
Hove, East Sussex, BN3 1JD, England.

British Library Cataloguing in Publication Data
St. Pierre, Meg
My Buddhist Life – (Everyday Religion)
1. Buddhism – Juvenile literature 2. Buddhists – Juvenile literature
I. Title II. Casey, Marty
294.3

ISBN 0-7502-1303-5

Picture acknowledgements

The authors and publishers thank the following for giving permission to reproduce
photographs: Chapel Studios 22; Clear Vision Trust 4, 5, 6, 7, 8, 9, 10, 11, 13, 14,
15, 16, 17, 18, 20, 25; Eye Ubiquitous 23, 26; Impact 24;
Panos Pictures 4; Ann & Bury Peerless 12, 21; Wayland Picture Library 19, 27.

Typeset by Joyce Chester
Printed in Italy by G Canale & S.p.A.

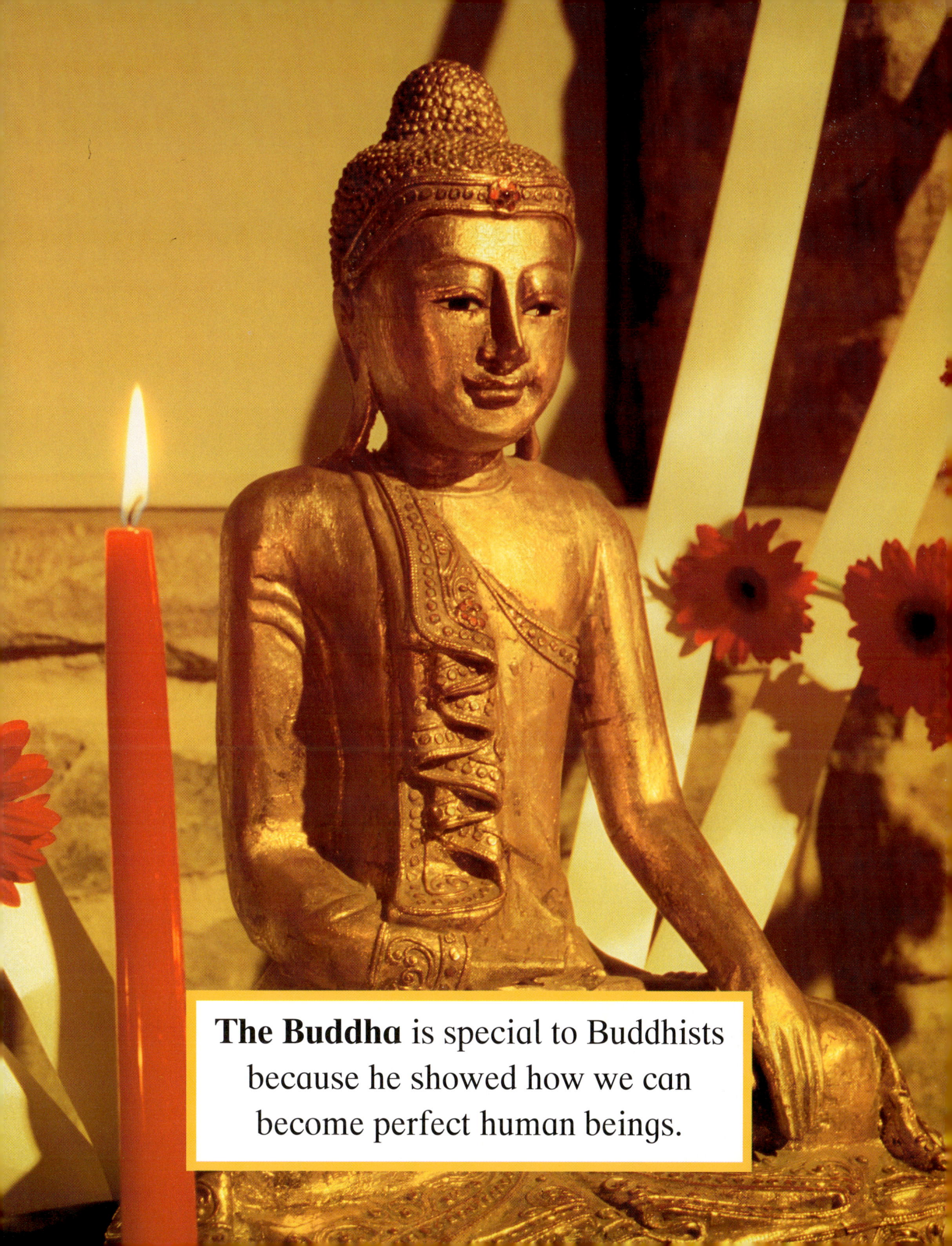

The Buddha is special to Buddhists because he showed how we can become perfect human beings.

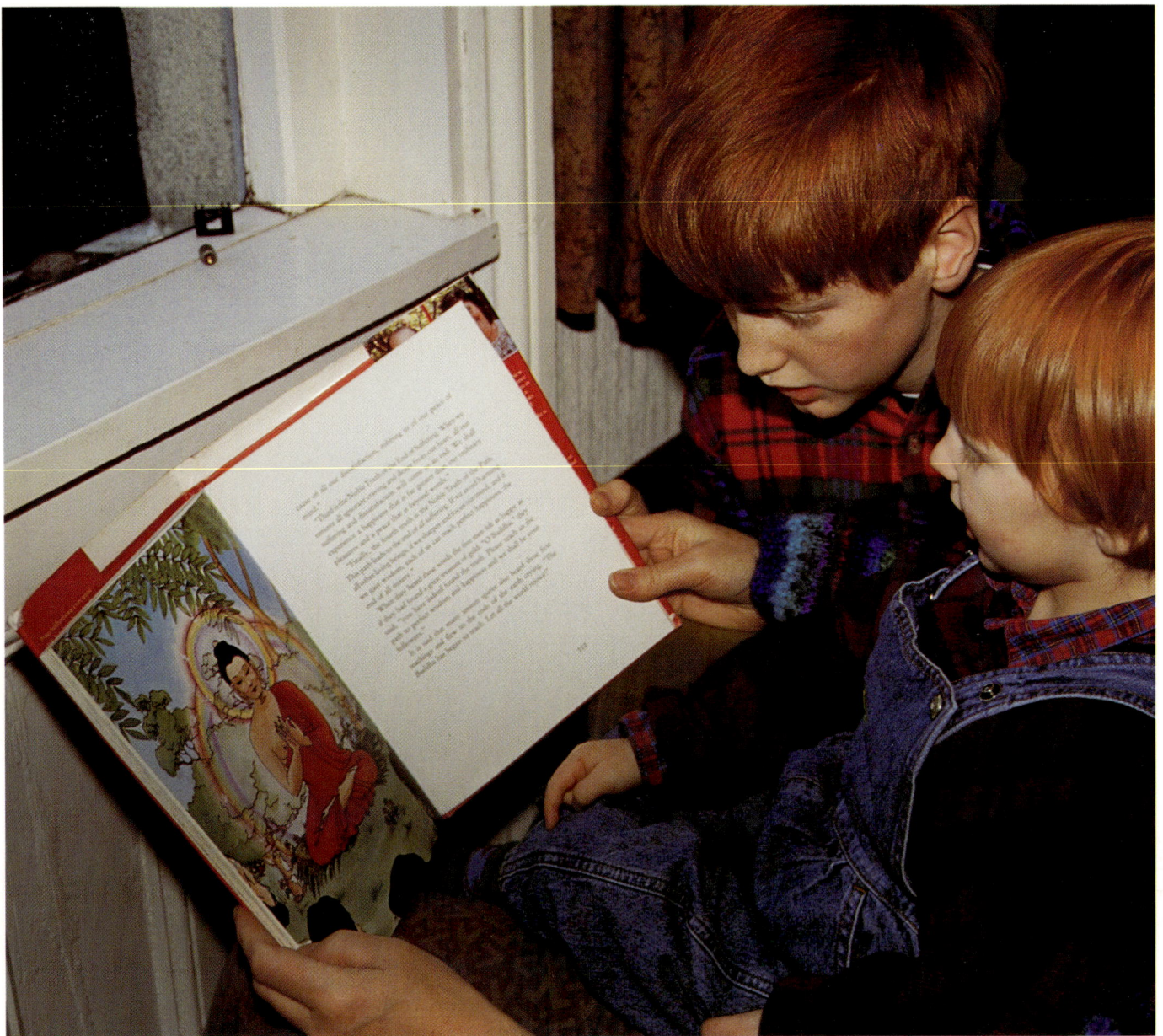

Ben likes to read stories about the Buddha to his brother. The Buddha was once an Indian Prince. He set out to find why there is unhappiness in the world and how to end it.

Sometimes Laura wonders about the unhappiness in the world.

Buddhists believe that the Buddha became **Enlightened**. He found out the Truth. He discovered the answer to unhappiness.

The Buddha was a wise and kind teacher. He taught people how to be happy. This special teaching is called the **Dharma**.

This beautiful statue is in Sri Lanka.
It was made long ago.
The Buddha's hands are resting
in his lap. This shows that he
is **meditating**.

Jaya is making a model.
She wants to show how kind and
brave the Buddha was.

This boy is reading about the Buddhist **precepts**. These are special guidelines for living that the Buddha taught.

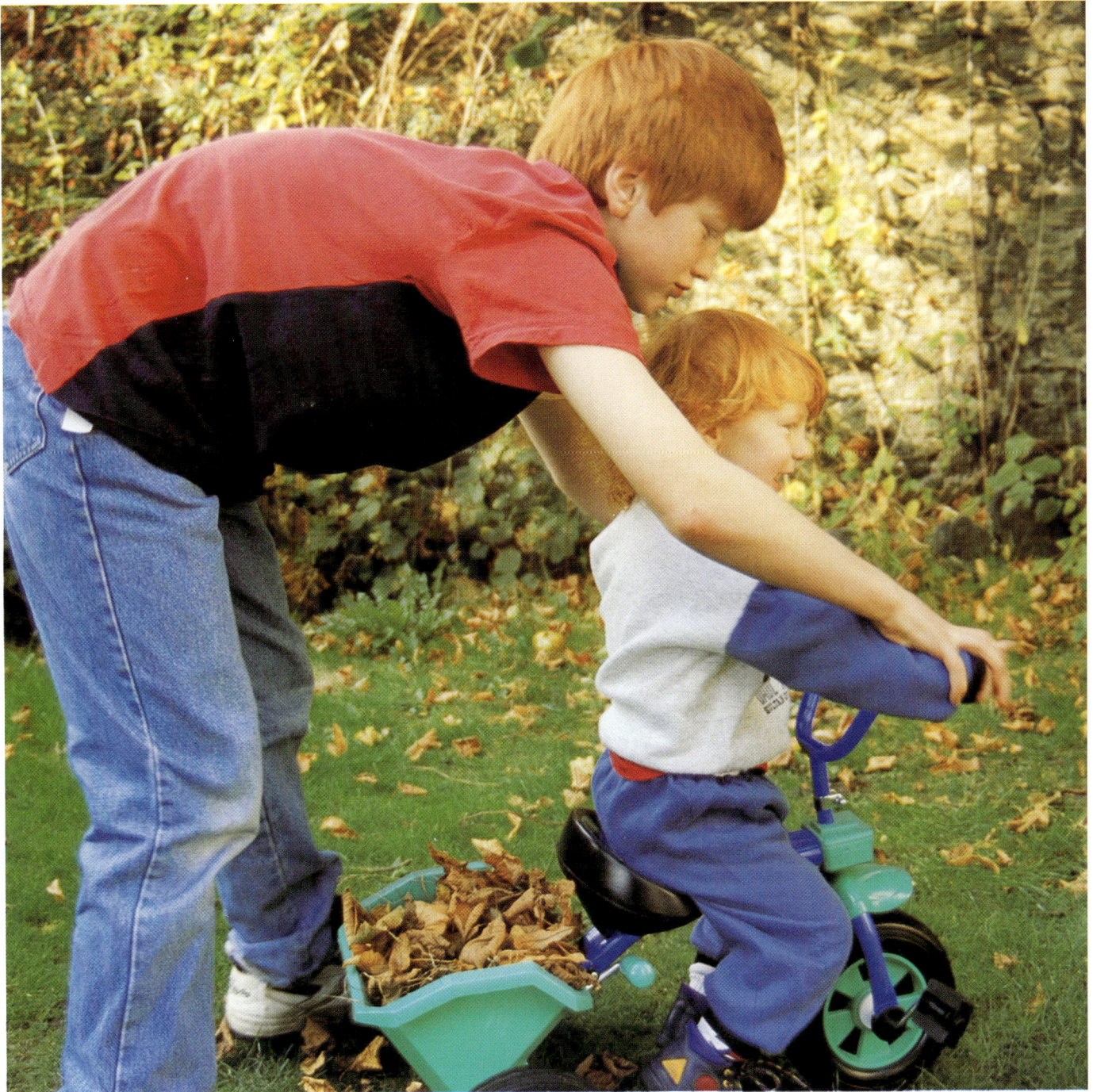

The most important precept is
not to harm living beings, but to
help them.

Annie likes to say thank you for the
teachings of the Buddha.

Buddhists all over the world chant special words. These words remind them of the Buddha and his teaching.

Sarah's mum is sitting very still and quiet. She is meditating. Meditation helps her to become a better person.

Sometimes Laura likes to be very
still and quiet too.

Everyone who lives by the Buddha's teaching is part of the **Sangha**.
They all belong to one big family.

For Buddhists it is very important to be good friends. Friends help each other to live a Buddhist life.

These monks are friends. They live together in a monastery. They are part of the Sangha.

Sarawanee and Uthen live in Thailand. They are part of the Sangha. They help the monks by giving them food and clothes.

At **Wesak** everyone enjoys remembering the Buddha's life. These people are celebrating the festival of Wesak.

This little boy is lighting lamps for the Wesak festival.

Suwat is eight. He lives in a monastery in Bangkok. He is training to be a monk.

Laura is also eight. Her mum and dad are Buddhists. She wants to be a Buddhist when she is older.

These friends know that it is very important to live a kind and helpful life.

May everything that lives be well!
Weak or strong, large or small,
seen or unseen, here or elsewhere,
present or to come, in heights or depths,
may all be well!

Notes for Teachers

Page 4 The Buddha lived 2,500 years ago in what is now north-east India and Nepal. Within a 100 years his teaching had spread all over India. Over the centuries, Buddhism spread throughout Asia, into such countries as Sri Lanka, Thailand, Cambodia, Burma, China, Japan and Tibet. Wherever it established itself, Buddhism adapted to the local culture. Buddhism spread to the West about 100 years ago. The major Easter traditions established themselves and new Western forms also developed. Worldwide, there are about 300 million Buddhists.

Page 5 The Buddha was not a god. For Buddhists there is no god. The Buddha was a human being who perfected himself and so went beyond being an ordinary person. He understood how things really are; he became Enlightened. He became a Buddha. All Buddhists believe that everyone who really tries can gain Enlightenment (reach Nirvana).

Page 6 Prince Siddhartha (who was to become the Buddha) was born about 560 BC. He lived a princely life and grew up in a palace. One day Siddhartha saw four sights which changed his life. He saw a sick person, a very old person and a dead person being carried in a funeral procession. The next day he saw a wandering holy man who looked peaceful and happy. Prince Siddhartha felt that there must be a solution to the problem of human suffering. He decided to leave his comfortable home and devote his life to finding the answer.

Page 7 Ask pupils to talk about a time when they have been happy and a time when they have been sad or upset. When they are unhappy, what can help them to become happy again? Can they think of other people who are happy? Can they think of people, or animals, who are unhappy or suffering? What could they do to help? Encourage the children to see how kindness helps others become happy.

Page 8 Siddhartha spent many years in the jungle trying to find an answer to the problem of suffering and unhappiness. He practised various austerities, such as fasting for long periods, but they didn't help him to get any closer to the answer. One day, he decided to sit down under a tree and meditate. He meditated all night, and by the morning he knew he had found the answer. He had become Enlightened, he had become a Buddha ('Buddha' means 'the one who is awake to the Truth').

Page 9 The Buddha was filled with compassion for human suffering and decided to devote himself to teaching others how to gain Enlightenment. For forty years he travelled over northern India, teaching all sorts of people, from kings and queens, to housewives, farmers, children, and even robbers. He taught that all beings can gain Enlightenment if they make the effort. The Name for the Buddha's teaching is the Dharma. The word Dharma also means the Truth.

Page 10 Statues and paintings of the Buddha remind Buddhists that they too can become Enlightened. All over the world there are Buddha images, from huge statues, to carved miniatures and paintings on cloth. Point out to the children how calm the face is on this statue. The eyes are closed, the mouth gently smiling. Some of the qualities of the Buddha are expressed in special hand positions called mudras.

Page 11 Ask children to talk about people they like. What is it about them that they like or admire? Possibly make a class list of good qualities such as generosity, kindness, etc. Suggest to the children that they draw or make a model of someone showing these qualities.

Page 12 Buddhists follow special guidelines for living, called the training precepts.

The Five Precepts

1. To avoid harming living beings and instead to practise helping others.

2. To avoid stealing and instead to practise being generous.

3. To avoid hurting others through being greedy and instead to practise contentment (this precept deals specifically with sexual conduct).

4. To avoid telling lies and instead to practise truthful speech.

5. To avoid taking alcohol or drugs and instead to keep the mind clear.

Buddhists try to live this way in order to become more like a Buddha, who would naturally act in this way.

Page 13 Encourage the children to think of ways they could become kinder. Who could we be kind to? How can we show kindness? Who do we know who is kind? How does kindness show?

Page 14 Buddhist worship is called puja. Buddhists worship in order to express their positive feelings, especially joy, gratitude, reverence and confidence. During the puja, special offerings of flowers, candles and incense are made. Flowers are offered to make the shrine beautiful, but they are also a reminder that everything changes and passes away. The candles are a symbol of Enlightenment – the Buddha's Enlightenment and the Buddhists' own future Enlightenment. The smell of incense, which spreads to fill the whole room, is a symbol that good actions have an effect on the world.

Page 15 Buddhists pay special reverence to the Buddha, the Dharma (the teaching) and the Sangha (the followers of the teaching). They refer to these as the Three Jewels, or the Three Refuges. Buddhists all over the world chant the Refuges and Precepts. Chanting the Precepts reminds Buddhists that what really matters is how they live their lives.

Page 16 Many Buddhists meditate every day. To meditate, they sit in an upright and comfortable position, so that they are relaxed yet alert. They then close their eyes and gently follow the movement of the breath as it goes in and out. Doing this helps develop calmness and concentration. Other meditations develop feelings of kindness towards self and others.

Page 17 Ask the children to talk about times when they have been still and quiet. Where do they go if they want to be quiet? Do they have a special quiet place or time? Children could practise a few moments of just sitting quietly and comfortably. They could imagine being in a beautiful quiet place. Afterwards talk about how it felt.

Page 18 The Sangha is the community of all those who practise the Buddha's teaching. Whatever tradition they follow, whether they are monk, nun, or lay-person, all are members of the Sangha.

Page 19 One very important aspect of Sangha is friendship. Buddhists know that friends can help each other along the path to Enlightenment. Some Buddhist traditions have a special Sangha day festival. Ask the children to talk about how friends can help each other.

Page 20 From the early days, some of the Buddha's followers wanted to spend all their time practising his teaching. They lived together in the forest, shaved their heads and wore simple robes. These were the first Buddhist monks and nuns. The monks and nuns of different traditions can be distinguished by the colour of their robes.

Page 21 Many of the Buddha's followers practised his teaching whilst living at home with their families. These were known as the lay followers. They help the monks and nuns by giving them food. Buddhists of the Theravada tradition give food to the monks and nuns as a way to practise generosity.

Page 22 Buddhists enjoy coming together for festivals. Each tradition has developed its own calendar of festivals. The most important festival celebrates the Buddha. It is usually celebrated on the full moon day of the month of May. Within the Theravada tradition, this festival is known as Wesak. Many Western Buddhists celebrate it as Buddha Day.

Page 23 The three things traditionally offered to the Buddha are flowers, incense and light. The shrine is usually the focal point of Buddhist worship. Chanting the Refuges and Precepts in front of the shrine, would be part of a festival day worship.

Page 24 Buddhism is part of cultural life for many people in Asia. Children are introduced into the Buddhist Sangha as babies. In some countries, young boys and girls may go and live in monasteries. Some return to their families after a while, others stay on and become ordained as monks and nuns.

Page 25 In the West, Buddhist parents bring their children up to follow the five precepts. When they are old enough, the children decide for themselves if they want to live the Buddhist life.

Page 26 For Buddhist parents the most important thing they can teach their children is how to be kind and considerate to people, animals and the environment. For this reason many Western Buddhists are vegetarian.

Page 27 This is a teaching of the Buddha called the Metta Sutta. This sutta expresses the important principle of kindness and compassion.

Glossary

The Buddha The one who is awake to the truth. The Buddha lived a long time ago in India. He spent many years teaching people to become Enlightened.

The Dharma The teaching of the Buddha. This teaching is now written down in special books. The Dharma also means the Truth.

Enlightenment The Buddha gained Enlightenment. An Enlightened person is perfectly wise and kind.

meditating Thinking about something deeply.

precepts Guidelines, or rules for living that are followed by Buddhists.

Sangha All those who follow the teaching of the Buddha are members of the Sangha, or community.

Wesak One of the names for the festival of the Buddha. This festival is celebrated in May. Wesak, or Vaisakhi, is the name of the Indian month of May.

Further Information

Books to Read

For Children
The Birth of the Buddha by Owen Cole and Judith Lowndes, Heinemann, 1995.
An illustrated book that tells the story of the young prince who was later to become the Buddha.

Jataka Tales by Abbie Blum and Lynn Dremalas, Dharma Publishing, 1992.
Stories of the past lives of the Buddha. Each of the nineteen stories has a moral theme.

Buddhism (World Religion series) by Catherine Hewitt, Wayland, 1995.

For Teachers
Introducing Buddhism by Chris Pauling, Windhorse Books, 1993.
Very readable and clear guide for teachers of all key stages.

Principles of Buddhism, Thorsons, 1996.
Teachers' guide to the key ideas at the heart of Buddhism.

Multimedia
Buddhism for Key Stage 2, The Clear Vision Trust.
A complete video resource pack, containing delightful stories which are suitable for infant pupils.

Index